The Provider's Guide to Leveraging "Obamacare"

Shaun Kirk, MHS, PT, MTC

Includes Bonus Chapters:

**The "Healthcare Practitioner Transition Plan" &
The "Obamacare Timeline"**

*To help you survive and prosper
through this new healthcare reform*

The author and publisher have made every effort to provide accurate information concerning the Patient Protection and Affordable Care Act and its potential impact and influence on healthcare service provider businesses; however, the Patient Protection and Affordable Care Act has been and may continue to be amended and revised as it moves through the implementation process.

For general information on our other products and services please contact our Customer Care Department at info@healthnetpublishing.com.

Edited by Rudi C. Loehwing

Cover design by Margie Rosenstein

Layout by DocUmeant Designs, DocUmeantDesigns.com

First Edition
ISBN13: 978-0-692-29052-1
ISBN10: 0-692-29052-4

Dedication

A tribute to Healthcare Practitioners throughout the United States.

Independent clinical practices are constantly challenged by governmental regulations and at every turn they persevere. There is little assistance for them. I would like to dedicate this book to the thousands of private practitioners who have a very powerful purpose to help improve the health and therefore the lives of millions of Americans.

This book is also dedicated to my wife for her support and encouragement along the way, and to my business partner, with whom none of this would have been possible.

Contents

1

Introduction

Hi, I'm Shaun Kirk, Co-founder and CEO of Measurable Solutions, Inc.

As a private practice physical therapist for many years and a successful business consultant to a range of businesses, clinics and service providers, I've taken quite a bit of time to study the Affordable Care Act as it is going to affect the healthcare industry and every one of us one way or another.

Healthcare reform is a moving target with changes happening almost every week. In fact, if you Google it, there will usually be quite a few news stories every day on the Affordable Care Act. It doesn't matter what side of the aisle you happen to be on it's no longer a political issue, it's a reality.

Despite the enormous volume of conversations and media coverage, many of our clients have told us that they haven't felt, or experienced, much of an impact in their practices so far and this may be the same for you.

Truthfully though, many private practitioners still have their head in the sand. They don't see the warning signs and are not preparing themselves and their clinics to deal with the "freight train" that is soon to plow its way into their practices.

We completed a national study of private practice clinicians to find out what their most immediate concerns were and yes, you probably guessed it . . .

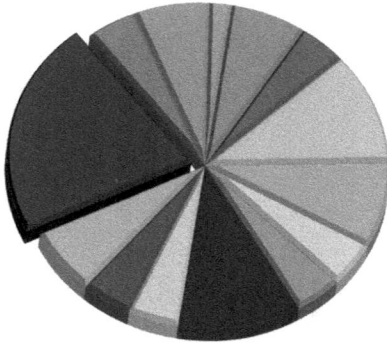

Obamacare came up as the number one concern across the boards. These clinicians and business owners were mainly worried about how Obamacare would impact their patient visit volume, the quality of care they are currently able to deliver to their patients, their collections and reimbursements and the additional paperwork that would soon be required.

Unfortunately, many practitioners have adopted a *"wait and see what happens"* attitude without making any preparations or appropriate changes in their operations *now* for what is sure to happen in the short and long-term future.

Regardless of your position or understanding of Obamacare and despite all of the confusion, hiccups in implementation, those countless changes that seem to be occurring each week and however it eventually shakes out, there are five key things that *will* happen:

1. You will be paid less per visit due to lowering patient visit rates and further reduced reimbursements.

2. Patients will be paying more because of the much higher deductibles in their new health insurance plans.

3. You will have to become very good at selling your services to secure stronger plan-of-care commitments since your patients are now going to have to pay more out of pocket for their care.

4. You'll also have to make up the difference with increased *new* patient volume.

5. And, all of your clinicians and staff will have to become even more productive and *much* more efficient.

The Affordable Care Act is a significant game changer and how you did things in the past may not bring about the stability and viability you'll need in the future. I believe that you should be fully prepared and taking action NOW in order to protect and continue to grow your practice because those five key things noted are certain to happen.

There is quite a bit to know about this particular law and how it may impact you as a clinician and employer, with your ability to recruit new staff, and even your overall profitability.

This is going to be a wake-up call for many healthcare practice owners. The implementation of Patient Protection and Affordable Care Act has been changed or altered nearly every day, but the fact remains that there are more people who are getting older, Medicare is going broke and the only way to make Medicare work is to pay you less per visit as time goes on.

I'm not trying to be the person who states doom and gloom, but I do want to increase your understanding of what is right in front of you. In California, several years ago, when Workers Compensation made some dramatic changes in its reimbursement policy many private practice owners were hit quite hard. These practice owners saw the handwriting on the wall, but did not take appropriate action to weather that storm and were thrust upon the rocks. Let's get ready for the future—NOW!

I'm hearing more and more chatter on things like Facebook and LinkedIn about how healthcare practitioners need to start moving towards cash-based practices and completely get out of the insurance game. My company was banging that drum six years ago, but got very few takers.

The truth of the matter is that most practice owners are very much entrenched in the insurance game and can fall victim to how they change the game. For example, if Blue Cross were to reduce their reimbursement by 10% or 20%, the likelihood is that most practice owners would just "take it." But, when all carriers reduce their reimbursement by 20%, then things start to really get frightening.

If I owned an insurance company and I believed in profits over care the best way to achieve that would be to reduce total case payout by simply raising the deductible for the patient.

If you've taken time to go on the Insurance Marketplace and look at the various insurance plans you would find that the deductibles are very high. Lucky for us, the insurance company and our government has shown us their cards. They stated specifically and directly via the Affordable Care Act what the intention of insurance in the future will become.

> *Insurance in the future is going to be one where the patient will have a larger out-of-pocket expense so that they will ONLY get the care that they absolutely feel they MUST have. By simply raising the out-of-pocket, the patient's condition will likely become far worse before they will act.*

Medicare reimbursement, although declining, is also being denied more and more.

The questions to ask yourself are:

> "Are my patients discharging me prior to achieving their goals for therapy because of their out-of-pocket expense being too high?"

> "Do I have an effective marketing program that gets new patients in the door?"

> "Do I know how to ask for and get patients referring friends and family in the volume I need?"

> "Do I know the real dollar value of each staff member to this organization and what I can do to improve their value and thus the viability of my company?"

These are the important questions that you should be asking yourself and focusing on this year and in the years to come. Effective and efficient improvements in these specific areas will make all the difference.

No matter what happens in the future with the Affordable Care Act, you need to know that YOU create your own personal economy. Your economy is not created elsewhere. You'll find, even in these trying times there are always organizations that thrive. The main difference between them and others is that they persevered. They researched and found out what to do and stringently applied that knowledge.

I would suggest that you do the same.

By finding and implementing solutions and not focusing or having fixed attention on the problems themselves you will be able to successfully weather any storm, and here is the litmus test for your practice;

> Walk into your organization tomorrow with the idea that every new patient from now on will have a $5000 deductible. I bet that your organization would change rapidly. My advice to you is start thinking that way now and acting as though it's that way already and when it does happen you will be not only still standing, but thriving and quite possibly buying out the practices of guys who failed to do so.

Now, let's take a look at the Affordable Care Act in some detail.

2

The Patient Protection and Affordable Care Act (PPACA)

Obamacare is truly one of the most significant "game changers" affecting our industry to date. The document itself is 2,700 pages long so I will focus on some of the most pertinent issues and situations that it creates for this industry so that you are pretty well briefed on them and can better understand how they will impact your practice.

Far more important to me; however, is that you are also able to do some things more effectively and successfully with the information that I provide.

The actual name of this Act is the Patient Protection and Affordable Care Act and you'll hear it called ACA, the Affordable Care Act and even Obamacare, which may have been a derogatory term when it was first coined, but has since gone on to become an iconic hallmark of the Barack Obama Presidential legacy.

Signed into law on March 23, 2010 it was fiercely contested, but upheld by the Supreme Court on June 28, 2012. This new healthcare law had the stated intention to provide health insurance coverage to roughly 44 million people who were said to be uninsured in the United States and its initial costs were estimated to be around $940 billion dollars.

Now that cost estimate has already been blown out of the water. It's apparently going to cost quite a lot more. If you know the history of Medicare, when it was signed into law in July 1965 the projected costs were off by as much as 12 times their initial estimates. So, we can probably take for granted that this new healthcare reform system is going to cost a lot more than initially estimated as well.

3
Obamacare: What Is It?

Obamacare mandates insurance coverage. This means that it has now become U.S. law that everyone *has to have* health insurance. Either they get it from their employer or they pay for it themselves.

It also expands Medicaid, which was created by the Social Security Amendments of 1965 as an entitlement program to help states provide medical coverage for low income families and other categorically related individuals who meet eligibility requirements. Candidates include the blind, aged, disabled and pregnant women. In essence, Medicaid serves as the nation's primary source of health insurance coverage for low-income populations. Medicaid is the largest existing source of funding for medical and health-related services for people with low income in the United States. The Patient Protection and Affordable Care Act significantly expanded both eligibility for and federal funding of Medicaid.

It also regulates insurance terms; how and what types of health insurance can be sold to the American public. Administratively, it created a Health Insurance Exchange also known as an Insurance Marketplace, which is the online site that people will go and obtain health insurance if it is not already being provided by their employers.

It subsidizes health insurance premiums for low-income people. You may be surprised what the new definition for "low-income" is now.

It then attempts to control healthcare costs via reimbursement reform, which is basically a code word for; "providers will be getting less money."

4

Revenue to be Generated to Pay for Obamacare

The money to pay for the estimated $1.2 trillion dollars behind Obamacare is supposed to come from the following areas:

$455 billion will come from Medicare cuts

$414 billion from the new taxes and fees

$349 billion from other, currently unspecified sources.

Whether you have a health insurance plan right now through your company or you have one individually, as of 2014 you will be personally paying $63.00 each year to the government, over and above your new premium payments, to help fund Obamacare and offset the cost of insuring people with medical problems.

Companies that do provide healthcare plans to their employees will also have to pay an additional $63.00 for every employee in a group health insurance plan. *So, for example, if you have 50 people in a group health plan, it will cost the company an additional $3,150.00 on top of the existing premiums.*

Obamacare *optimistically* proposes to raise its own funding, which will be roughly $1.2 billion dollars over the next 10 years, through a series of no less than 21 brand new taxes and fees that we will actually see being implemented.

The 21 (NEW) Tax Increases

Individual Mandate Excise Tax—for anyone who does not buy "qualifying" health insurance

Employer Mandate Tax—officially referred to as a "shared responsibility payment," to help fund marketplace subsidies and fund other aspects of the Affordable Care Act

A new 3.8% Surtax on Investment Income

Excise Tax on Comprehensive Health Insurance; Plans—in 2018 a 40% excise tax added to premium health plans

Hike in Medicare Payroll Tax—2.9 to 3.8%

Medicine Cabinet Tax—no longer possible to purchase non-prescription drugs from their Health savings accounts

HSA Withdrawal Tax Hike—10- to 20% increase for non-medical early withdrawals from HSA accounts

Flexible Savings Account Cap—imposes a cap on FSAs of $2,500 (it was "unlimited" until 2013). Note: This provision is especially cruel to parents of special needs children

Elimination of tax deductions for employer-provided retirement prescription drug coverage

Blue Cross / Blue Shield Tax Hike—85% or more of premiums that are not spent on clinical services

Excise Tax on Charitable Hospitals—$50,000 tax if new rules are not met

Tax on Innovator Drug Companies—$2.3 billion annual tax imposed relative to share of annual drug sales

Tax on Heath Insurers—annual tax relative to annual insurance premiums collected

$500,000 Annual executive compensation limit for Health Insurance executives

Employer Reporting of Insurance on W-2—a preamble to taxing health benefits on individual tax returns

Corporate 1099-MISC Information Reporting—forgone tax revenues lost in provision repeals will be offset by a $24.882 billion increase in the amount of health insurance subsidies that will need to be paid back to the Treasury by Americans living at or near the poverty line

Tax on Medical Device Manufacturers—a new 2.3% excise tax on medical device manufacturers as of 2013

"Black Liquor" Tax Hike—bio-fuel tax

"Haircut" for Medical Itemization Deduction—raises the threshold that unreimbursed medical and dental expenses you paid for yourself, your spouse, and your dependents must reach before a deduction is permitted

Codification of the "Economic Substance Doctrine"—enables the IRS to arbitrarily disallow legally valid deductions that it deems the action "lacks substance" and is merely intended to reduce taxes

New 10% Tax on Americans using indoor tanning salons

5
Obamacare: What Does It Do?

So, what does Obamacare do?

- It makes healthcare much more accessible for a lot of people.

- It eliminates "pre-existing conditions" as the reason for health insurance companies to refuse to underwrite health insurance policies or add exorbitant fees to their premiums, which they used to be able to do.

- It should create more demand for healthcare services since more people will be able to get health insurance that couldn't before and they will now be more interested in a wider range of healthcare services.

- And it provides a broader alternative to the employer-based health insurance business model.

Up until now you had just a few ways to get health insurance in this country. You could get it through your employer or you could get it individually. When you went to get it individually, your premium was based on your health history and a number of other factors and then insurance companies could just say that they didn't want to insure you.

As a practice owner you should also be aware that there is a lot of experimentation within Obamacare in an effort to move from the "fee-for-service" model for reimbursing healthcare providers over to a more "outcome-oriented" or "results-oriented" type of system.

Even today it's still not well defined, but it is definitely coming.

6
So, Who Is Affected?

The first question that came to mind with many Americans upon passage of the Affordable Care Act was; "how will it affect me, my family, and my business?"

The honest answer was and still is that it really depends on a number of factors including personal and household incomes and whether or not you currently have health insurance.

Pretty much everybody is or will be affected!

If you are a U.S. citizen, you're either getting taxed more on your health insurance or you'll be getting subsidized. If you're a healthcare provider you're either winning or feeling the crunch more than ever.

It affects pretty much
EVERYBODY!

7
How Will Universal Coverage Be Achieved?

Up till now, if you worked for a large company then you may have obtained some form of group health insurance from your employer. If you were over 65 then Medicare covered you. If you were in a low-income bracket then Medicaid covered you. Otherwise you went out and got your own individual health insurance policy and yet, even with that about 44 million Americans didn't have their own health insurance.

So, the way they're going to level the playing field on health insurance is this;

> Health insurance premiums will be subsidized and the plans that are available from the new Insurance Marketplace will look quite like the group insurance plans that the big insurance companies have been selling to businesses.

Now as an individual, you can go to the Marketplace and get your own health insurance policy and it will look just like it would if you were buying it from an insurance company directly . . . and it will be guaranteed. You won't have to fill out any health forms or anything like that, you'll just get it.

Obamacare will also expand Medicaid to cover more and more people.

This is huge, because this is how the administration plans to cover about 21 million more people who are currently without health insurance. The plan is to raise the level that Medicaid covers to include people that didn't qualify for Medicaid in the past.

Then Obamacare will mandate large companies to either provide health insurance coverage or pay significant "fines."

Obamacare will also mandate that each citizen, not covered by an employer group plan, must purchase their health insurance or pay a "fine." The reason why I used the words "fines" and "fine" in quotation marks here is because that's how the original Patient Protection and Affordable Care Act, was written until it went to the Supreme Court. The way that the Supreme Court rationalized Obamacare and found it to be *Constitutional* is that they determined that it could not be called a "fine" as that would make the mandate premise unconstitutional. So, they decided to call it a "tax."

Therefore, because the government has the right to "tax" its citizens, the mandate provision of Obamacare was now quite easily made fully "constitutional"—a premise that will probably be debated for many years to come.

In any case, it's really just the semantics or a word game, but that's how Obamacare became law, constitutionally.

For businesses that are required to provide health insurance to their employees, the threshold is a company with 50 FTEs (full-time employees) requires them to provide group health insurance. However, the definition of "full-time employee" has been changed by Obamacare. It is not quite what you may have considered a full-time employee to be up till now. I'll tell you more about that in a little bit.

8
The Health Insurance Marketplace

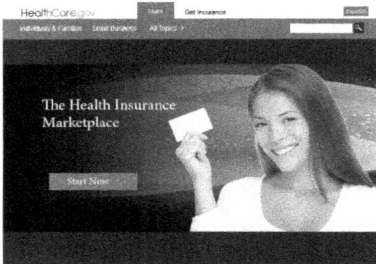

I want to cover this new *Health Insurance Marketplace* because this is the "Magilla Gorilla" of Obamacare. This is the very thing that is going to change everything.

The Marketplace is a set of government-regulated and standardized private healthcare plans currently available online if you can get the web site to stay up and running long enough. Open enrollment began on October 1, 2013 and it took effect in January, 2014.

It's located on a website. https://www.healthcare.gov.

You simply go on to the web site and as you go through the initial process you may begin to think that you are filling out your tax forms. You first have to put all of your personal information in and then all of your entire household's income information so that they can figure out what subsidies you may now qualify for.

After you get through all the tax type information and if the web site is still working that day you'll be able to go and look at the health insurance plans that are available and you can pick a plan that works for you.

Basically, there are four levels of health insurance plans and, depending on your state, you may find that all the major companies will be participating. So, there will be companies like BlueCross, there will be Aetna, United, etc. While they are private insurance companies, the plans themselves will be regulated and standardized by the government.

So, at this point there's really no difference between Blue Cross or Aetna or United, when it comes to what they can provide. That's why the insurance companies are basically going to be turned into utility companies, because the only differentiation will really be how efficient they are in making money, their customer service and things like that. They're not going to have much latitude to provide "this" benefit instead of "that" benefit, because the government has already decided what benefits are going to be in there.

When you buy health insurance through the Marketplace, the only way they differentiate the premium you will pay is based on your age and your geography. A person with diabetes or a heart condition or anything like that would pay the same as a marathon runner at age 25 when it comes to their premiums. There's no more medical underwriting. There's no longer any risk assessment as to who's more likely to cost insurance companies more money.

Inevitably, the costs of all insurance will have to go up, because now it has to cover the costs of all those people that the insurance companies had been excluding all these years.

9
Essential Health Benefits

There are ten categories of *"Essential Health Benefits,"* and *"Rehab Services"* are also in there, which is a good thing for all of us.

Every plan will have these elements which mirror most existing group plans as well, and most of the insurance terms will also be the same. So, even if you are a big company and you get a big group plan from Blue Cross this is what that would look like.

All private health insurance plans offered in the Marketplace will offer the same set of essential health benefits, which include at least the following items and services:

- Ambulatory patient services (outpatient care you get without being admitted to a hospital)

- Emergency services

- Hospitalization (such as surgery)

- Maternity and newborn care (care before and after your baby is born)

- Mental health and substance use disorder services, including behavioral health treatment (this includes counseling and psychotherapy)

- Prescription drugs

- Rehabilitative and habilitative services and devices (services and devices to help people with injuries, disabilities, or chronic conditions gain or recover mental and physical skills)

- Laboratory services

- Pediatric services

- Preventive and wellness services and chronic disease management.

Preventive health services for adults

Most health plans must cover a set of preventive services like shots and screening tests at no cost to you. This includes Marketplace private insurance plans.

Free preventive services

All Marketplace plans and many other plans must cover the following list of preventive services without charging a co-payment or co-insurance. This is true even if you haven't met your yearly deductible. This applies only when these services are delivered by a network provider.

1. Abdominal Aortic Aneurysm one-time screening for men of specified ages who have never smoked

2. Alcohol Misuse screening and counseling

3. Aspirin use to prevent cardiovascular disease for men and women of certain ages

4. Blood Pressure screening for all adults

5. Cholesterol screening for adults of certain ages or at higher risk

6. Colorectal Cancer screening for adults over 50

7. Depression screening for adults

8. Diabetes (Type 2) screening for adults with high blood pressure

9. Diet counseling for adults at higher risk for chronic disease

10. HIV screening for everyone ages 15 to 65, and other ages at increased risk

11. Immunization vaccines for adults—doses, recommended ages, and recommended populations vary:

   - Hepatitis A
   - Hepatitis B
   - Herpes Zoster
   - Human Papillomavirus
   - Influenza (Flu Shot)
   - Measles, Mumps, Rubella
   - Meningococcal
   - Pneumococcal
   - Tetanus, Diphtheria, Pertussis
   - Varicella

12. Obesity screening and counseling for all adults

13. Sexually Transmitted Infection (STI) prevention counseling for adults at higher risk

14. Syphilis screening for all adults at higher risk

15. Tobacco Use screening for all adults and cessation interventions for tobacco users

Essential health benefits are the minimum requirements for all plans in the Marketplace. However, individual health insurance plans may offer additional coverage. You will see exactly what each plan offers when you compare them side-by-side in the Marketplace.

10
What Were the State Insurance "Exchanges?"

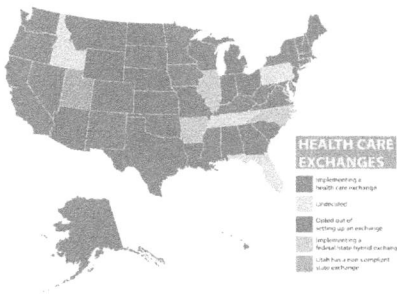

Early on, before it became law, while the current health-care reform was in its formative and even debate stages, you may have heard about the "State Exchanges." The way these exchanges were supposed to work was that each state was supposed to make their own. So, wherever you lived in the country, that state was supposed to create their own "Exchange of Insurance Marketplace" and you would go online within your State and go through the registration and insurance selection process.

When Obamacare went to the Supreme Court, while they did say that Obamacare was constitutional what they also said was that they couldn't force states to implement these Exchanges or Marketplaces. So, what's happened here is that a number of States decided that they would create their own Marketplaces and other states decided to let the Federal government handle it for them.

Either way, you won't see any difference when you log onto the Insurance Marketplace website to enroll or just check out the new insurance plans that are available.

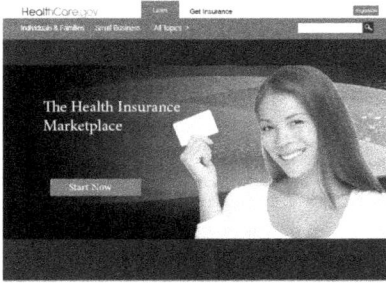

As previously noted, Obamacare open enrollment started on October 1, 2013. The health insurance Marketplace is located on a website: https://www.health-care.gov.

People fill out online forms to determine what subsidies they are entitled to and what plans they want to sign up for.

Private insurance companies will compete with their health insurance plans, but they will offer essentially the same benefits, though there are different levels of insurance coverage and deductibles.

People will choose a plan and, if they are eligible, they can get subsidies or maybe a tax credit to help pay their premiums.

11
Health Insurance Subsidies

HEALTH INSURANCE

★ APPROVED ★

EXCHANGE SUBSIDIES

The following spread sheet is your guide to the insurance premium subsidies. To demonstrate how this works, look at the first column, under "Household Size."

Let's look at number 1 of the Health Insurance Exchange Subsidies graphic.

We'll say you're a single person. If you look to next column to the right under the 100% of the poverty level, it is $11,490.00, which means that if you make $11,490.00 or less then you're officially at the poverty line.

This graph clearly shows that if you make that amount of money when you go to the Marketplace to get your health insurance, the maximum you can pay for your premium is 2% of your $11,490.00 income or, in this case, just $19.00 a month. The rest of the premium whatever it costs will be subsidized by the government.

So, let's say that your insurance costs $400.00 per month in the Exchange and you make $11,490, you'll wind up paying $19.00 each month and the government will pay $381.00 each month. That's a good deal, right?

Health Insurance Exchange Subsidies

% of Income Premium Limit -	2%	3%	4%	6%	9.5%	9.5%
Percent of Poverty Level -	100	133	150	200	300	400
Household size						
1	11,490	15,282	17,235	22,980	34,470	45,960
Max Monthly Premium -	$19	$38	$57	$116	$273	$364
2	15,510	20,628	23,265	31,020	46,530	62,040
Max Monthly Premium -	$26	$52	$78	$157	$368	$491
3	19,530	25,975	29,295	39,060	58,590	78,120
Max Monthly Premium -	$33	$65	$98	$197	$464	$618
4	23,550	31,322	35,325	47100	70,650	97200
Max Monthly Premium -	$39	$78	$118	$238	$559	$746
5	27,570	36,668	41,355	55140	82,710	110280
Max Monthly Premium -	$46	$92	$138	$279	$655	$873

Now, go to the end, all the way across to the last column where it shows $45,960.00. If you are a single person making $45,960.00, which is 400% of the poverty line, you would still qualify for a subsidy. The difference is that you can't pay more than 9.5% of your $45,960.00 income. So, you won't pay more than $364.00 a month and the government will pay the rest each month in a subsidy.

And then you are going to have choices for how rich your plan is. There are Bronze, Silver, Gold, and Platinum health insurance plans that will be available through the Marketplace. The difference is that the plans will cover 60%, 70%, 80% or 90% of your healthcare cost.

Your premium is going to be higher for the Platinum and lower for the others.

Using the same spreadsheet let's look at a family of five that earns $27,570.00 a year income. They'll only have to pay 2% of their income in health insurance premiums each month. So, they'll be paying $46.00 a month for their health insurance plan.

It costs about $1,300.00 a month for this family of five, but they'll pay $46.00 and the government will pay the rest.

This is HUGE!

The way this works with Obamacare is you have an individual person paying the $46.00 premium each month, so he writes a check for $46.00 to the insurance company and then the government writes a check and they also pay the insurance company on his behalf.

This is very important because you can see that we're not talking about subsidizing only lower-income here. When you go up to 400% of the Federal Poverty Line, you end up with a single person making $45,960 a year, but also getting subsidized in his health insurance. Subsidizing will do nothing but go up in cost because the poverty level goes up every year and these numbers will increase every year along with them.

And, I'll give you a little strategy in the "Solutions & Opportunities" section that will enable you to capitalize on this in your business. It is very important that you understand it.

12
State Medicaid & Medicare

How will this affect Medicaid & Medicare?

People up to 133% of the Federal Poverty Line can now get Medicaid, if the states agree.

Medicare payments to health-care providers are being reduced to help fund Obamacare. So, you're going to see a reduction this year in Medicare-provider funding.

This the way it works;

> The government will raise money by cutting reimburse-ments to healthcare providers, because allegedly, if you do that, then you are not really hurting the patients. But as a provider, you will have to absorb the difference. Nevertheless, it is totally expected that you will treat patients at the same level of care, but for less reimbursement.

Now you know that's not going to work, but that's the way the government expects it to.

The Independent Payment Advisory Board[1]

This is huge and it's already started, it's just now more of a *recommendation* type process, but this new agency is getting their sea legs.

Medicare is on a certain, somewhat controlled, growth path. However, if Medicare costs grow faster, then this Independent Payment Advisory Board will make recommendations to change things in order to bring those costs down.

A good example of this happened some time ago. The Board issued a recommendation that basically said that mammograms for women were no longer necessary in certain age groups. While this was merely the board's opinion and they had no real power, there was a public uproar over it.

That's just a little bit about what's likely going to happen and what you're likely going to see as the Board starts looking at certain procedures and the cost-effectiveness of them. For the first three years it won't really matter. They'll just publish their reports and recommendations and it will all be very interesting.

However in 2018 when the Board issues their cost-reducing recommendations they'll go to the U.S. Congress. Congress either has to vote against them with a three-fifths supermajority or the recommendations become new law.

You just can't create a Board and give them legislative power because it's unconstitutional. So, the government simply created this system where the Board's recommendations act as a "Bill" that goes to Congress. They then made it very difficult for Congress to vote against their recommendations because they've got to come up with three-fifths supermajority to do so.

It is very important to point out that this group will have a lot of power in the future when it comes to Medicare—and

---

1 Government Advisory Board (IPAB) to help control the growth in Medicare costs.

probably even rehabilitative care—because things that happen in Medicare tend to trickle down into everything else.

This Board could decide, for example, that it's not cost-effective to do a hip replacement after age "X" and this is where the fear of establishing those futuristic "death panels" came from. Currently, Britain has this in place. They have a Board that does this and they are making very tough choices.

So, what about Medicaid?

Now, another way that the government plans to fund Obamacare is by expanding Medicaid. Currently, every State has a different gauge or measure for the "poverty line" that qualifies its citizens for Medicaid and they all are within 60–70% of the federal poverty line.

What Obamacare tells the states is that they have a real "deal" for them. The administration wants each state to standardize their poverty line to 133% of the federal poverty line. Basically, they want each state to expand how much a person can make and still qualify for Medicaid.

And, if the states do it, then the government will pay 100% of the increased costs of doing so for the first three years and for the next seven years, they will pay 90% of those costs. So, it's essentially "free money" for the States to expand their Medicaid rolls.

So, why are so many states not on board for free money?

Well, there are really two basic reasons:

One of the main reasons is simply that they don't totally *trust* the Federal Government and think that they're likely to start this thing and then they are going to get squeezed.

And another reason is the lack of participation. In the State of Florida for example, only 65% of the people that actually qualify for Medicaid actually apply to get it. They've got 35% of their population who could get Medicaid, but don't even apply for whatever reason.

The fear is that the additional 35% that could have been getting Medicaid all along will now come in for it and the Feds
won't cover them because they were not included in the new
plan.

So, what the states are worried about is all these people that
for whatever reason, have stayed away from Medicaid, under
the new rules can get it now and will come into the system
and the States just won't have the money to pay for it.

The dilemma here is that if states don't adjust their own numbers according to the Federal Poverty Line levels it's going
to significantly limit the number of people that will get health
insurance in those states and we'll wind up with the same
problem that healthcare reform was supposed to address in
the first place!

We have 44 million people who don't have health insurance now and if all of the states don't get on board with the
Federal government's plan then we're still going to end up,
after Obamacare, with around 30 million people that still won't
have health insurance.

13
Medicare Advantage

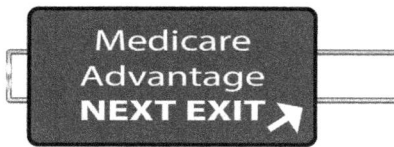

Medicare Advantage is the supplemental coverage for low-income citizens with private insurers.

The way it works is subscribers pay a certain amount of money and the insurance companies provide additional coverage on top of Medicare. The payoff is if the insurance companies can control their costs then they get to keep the difference between what they get and what they pay out.

Obamacare doesn't seem to like Medicare Advantage so they're going to hit the insurance companies when they think their medical loss ratio[2] is too high.

Essentially, they're saying that the insurance companies are making excessive profits with Medicare Advantage and the government is going to lower those profits. This will cut funding to Medicare Advantage and you're probably going to see Medicare Advantage fade away, eventually.

---

2 The proportion of premium revenues an insurer spends on claims and expenses that improve healthcare quality.

14
Employer's Choice

Employers with an average of 50 FTEs, which are full-time or full-time equivalent employees, is the demarcation line for this health insurance mandate.

In other words, if you're an employer that has less than 50 full-time employees or the equivalent, then the mandate doesn't apply to you and you *don't have to* provide health insurance coverage to any of your employees.

Now, if you do currently provide coverage for your employees then the plan you provide needs to meet the essential health benefits standard as dictated by Obamacare.

However, there is no mandate on you and no penalty for not doing so if you don't have 50 full-time or full-time equivalent employees. But, if you do have 50 FTEs then you will have to provide health coverage that is affordable and provides minimum value or you'll end up paying a tax.

The problem here is that Obamacare changed the definition for what a Full-Time Employee (FTE) is.

Most business owners consider a normal 40-hour work week to identify a full-time from a part-time employee. However, with Obamacare, a full-time employee or full-time equivalent is now a *30-hour per week* employee. The "magic number" for employers is 1500. The government could use this number to force employers with less than 50 actual employees to pay for health insurance for their employees because the total number of employee hours worked for the company is 1,500 or more each week (1500 work hours per week ÷ 30 hours per week = 50 FTEs or Full Time "Equivalent" employees).

Therefore, a company with 37.5 employees working 40 hours each week, (1,500 total work hours), would meet the criteria because a 30-hour work week is now considered full-time or full-time equivalent employee.

If your practice is in this range you may need to have a group plan for your employees, but you may also be able to take advantage of the Insurance Marketplace options as a solution to employee healthcare requirements. If you practice does have 50 or more FTEs you may also want to do everything possible to bring it under 50 FTEs if it is feasible.

This is very important and we were told by the Obama Administration that you needed to start calculating this number as of July 1, 2013. In other words, for 2014 your average FTEs between July 1, 2013 and the end of 2013, month-by-month, determines whether you have to adhere to the mandate and provide health insurance to your employees.

Of course, in an effort to reduce the impact of the Obamacare mandate financially you may be able to bring your part-time employees who have been working 30+ hours each week and maybe even some of your full-time employees down to 29.5 hours per week in order to avoid the mandate with them. Only you know if it would work with regards to managing, productivity and your business schedule. You'll certainly have to communicate with those employees so you don't inadvertently lose them. You may even have to adjust their hourly wage to make up for an unwanted pay cut, but you'll avoid having to cover their monthly insurance premiums.

In any event, you would only have to pay for the employees who are considered full-time or full-time equivalent. You may want to check with your CPA if this is an option for you.

If you already have a group insurance plan and you have less than 50 FTEs you're fine, but you could end that group insurance plan next year if you wanted to because there would be no mandate on you to have it. Now, you probably didn't do it because of a mandate, but the point is if you're over 50 FTEs then you *have to do it*.

And the IRS is the policing body on all of this. So, there'll be more reporting to the IRS as Obamacare rolls out.

The Affordability Test[3]

Healthcare coverage under Obamacare is considered by the administration to be "affordable" because the employee's own contribution to single coverage cannot be more than 9.5% of their adjusted gross *household* income.

If you are required to provide your employees with health insurance, then here is a word of caution; if just one person in your company fails this "affordability test" and goes to the Marketplace to get insurance, then you could end up paying up to $3,000.00 for every employee in your company, after 30 employees, as a penalty.

As an example; if you have 100 people in your company, for employee number 31 to employee number 100 you could end up paying as much as $2,000.00–$3,000.00 each. Again, you just have to have one person who fails the "affordability test" in your company for this to kick in. It's very important that you make sure that your insurance plan passes this "affordability test" if you do have a group health insurance plan. So, you will really need to stay on track with this.

What you're going to see here is that there are some fairly insidious motivations at work that all go to the same place. As a practitioner and as a business owner there's more and

---

3 Health insurance coverage is deemed to be affordable for the Patient Protection and Affordability Act purposes if the cost to the employee of *self-only coverage* does not exceed 9.5% of the employees "household income."

more of this that makes you feel like you'll need to get out of this group health insurance game, which is actually what the government appears to want you to do!

Minimum and Actuarial Value

There's also this concept called "Minimum Value" (MV) or "Actuarial Value" (AV), which is the proportion of medical expenses an insurance plan is expected to cover. An Actuarial Value of 100 means that a plan would pay 100% of all medical expenses.

Health Insurance Plans must cover at least 60% of the Actuarial Value of the plan's total cost, which is not the premium, it's the total cost of the plan itself.

So when you go to the Marketplace you'll see Bronze (60%), Silver (70%), Gold (80%) and Platinum (90%) type plans. They're all based on this "Actuarial Value." It's that the insurance covers 60% or 70% or 80% or 90% and the insured covers the rest in their deductibles and co-payments.

15

How Obamacare Will Affect Your Patients?

Theoretically, more payments via insurance carriers should seem to occur because more patients will now have insurance. However, due to significantly higher deductibles in the health insurance plans under Obamacare, patients may be required to make significant cash payments, which may cause unforeseen limits to patient visits as well as procedures and patients could wind up "discharging" you!

Physical Therapy and Occupational Therapy services will be more affordable and therefore they should be used more. The thing we have going for us here is that we are results-oriented and reasonably priced providers compared to a lot of services that insurance pays for. Chances are we're going to *get utilized more* and more because we're going to *get better outcomes at lower costs.*

This is what healthcare reform is all about!

The bottom line is that the government is subsidizing Physical Therapy and Occupational Therapy services through all of these activities and regulatory changes. It's going to increase your prospective patient's access, which is a good thing.

Access to services will no longer be discouraged by cost outside of insurance policy deductibles. There are people out there that would like to come to your clinic, but don't because to them it costs too much and they didn't have insurance coverage in the past. With such substantial subsidies, that shouldn't happen in the future.

Co-pays will likely rise for many existing and newly insured consumers as well. This could have significant impact on existing patient visits and patient plan of care completion numbers.

And then there are the outcome-oriented measures that are in Obamacare. These are the pilots that are going to lead towards more of the "documentation of progress" and pay-ments that are based on that.

Again, because of what we do, we're actually positioned well for this because there are a lot of things in the medical pro-fession that don't do very well with creating objective results. Chances are this could be a good thing for Physical Therapy and Occupational Therapy.

A word of warning: Due to other cost-cutting provisions within the structure and oversight of Obamacare, providers may-have to resort to cookie-cutter treatments resulting in lowered quality of care.

Let's not have that happen!

16
How Obamacare Will Affect Your Employees?

On average, healthcare benefit costs will continue to rise. Blue Cross, Aetna, United, they're all sending out the signals. You should expect premiums next year to go up between 25% and 50%. Every State has regulations on this and while there are some States that impose a "cap" on rising premium, it still remains that 25%–50% is what premiums are expected to rise.

What's happening here is that the higher level of "essential benefits" in the Obamacare list of health insurance plans is causing this increase in premiums. Insurance companies can no longer make money by excluding people. Now they've got more older people that are going to cost them a lot of money. So, the people that were already in the game are now going to have to pay a bit more money to cover for the people that have just joined the game.

Younger, healthier people will have to pay more. In the past, if you were a young person you could get a scaled-down health insurance plan for almost nothing because you may not have needed things like maternity coverage and this or that. You could do it "cafeteria-style," but you really can't do that anymore. Obamacare insurance plans have to have all of the "essential benefits."

However, low monthly premiums with high deductible "catastrophic" plans are also available on the insurance Marketplace for working singles under the age of 30 who don't have health insurance.

Basically, the Obamacare plans are like going to a car dealership and having to buy a Cadillac because they think Cadillacs are good, but they also cost a lot of money. So, the government's going to subsidize some of that and this is the way it kind of works.

Many people will lose their company group plans and the way they'll lose them is for business owners who decide that they are going to send their employees to the Marketplace and get out of the group insurance game altogether.

Lower income people will have their insurance premium costs capped. This group of insured people are the huge winners here. The earlier chart demonstrated that if a person was making $15,000.00 a year they would be getting their premium's subsidized by 85%—that's huge.

Think about it. A person could have diabetes and a heart condition and make $15,000.00 a year and still only have to pay about $20.00 a month for full health insurance.

The individual Mandate is going to force people to get insurance or eventually they are going to pay a fine (tax), but what they get in return is quite a bit.

They get guaranteed coverage, no medical underwriting, premium subsidies and maybe even tax credits.

Sounds like a pretty good deal?

17
How Obamacare Will Affect Your Practice?

So, how will this affect your practice as a business?

Reimbursement rates will certainly decrease. Except for Medicaid, if you do Medicaid, it's going up because when they expand Medicaid they're going to increase Medicaid reimbursements closer to Medicare reimbursements—at least for now.

There's going to be more paperwork and documentation required and you can probably bank on that.

Electronic Medical Records (EMRs) will continue to be big and it is not likely these will be simplified with Obamacare, if anything, they will likely get more complex.

The government claims that the Obamacare administration is going to be made simpler because it will be standardized. Well, we'll see.

You're going to have less revenue per patient, but potentially a lot more of them.

Demand for services will increase and potentially a lot more people should be coming in for service. Massachusetts is the closest little incubator to this. When this state put Romneycare in place, back in 2006, patient usage went through the roof. There's an old adage; "What you subsidize, you get more of."

Subsidize health insurance or healthcare and you get more people accessing healthcare.

This creates an expanded market opportunity. You're going to be marketing to people that couldn't afford your services earlier that now can, which should be exciting.

You should watch the Accountable Care Organizations (ACOs)[4] and see if they start up in your area. At some point, if these things become big, you're going to have to decide whether you're "in" or "out" because the more people and the more things that go into these ACOs, the more they become these closed "referral" facilities. You may not get anything from them unless you're one of the "insiders."

You can join them, but we know that the HMOs didn't work very well and it's entirely possible that ACOs aren't going to work either, but we'll see.

The status of Physical Therapy and Occupational Therapy as essential healthcare benefit providers will be directly related to perceived results-orientation and their ability to reduce overall healthcare costs. I think we all believe that they do and if they do then I think you're going to see us as the big winner's here.

On average, profit margins for healthcare providers as a per-cent of revenue will go down, but total profits could likely go up and this is why:

> Although your reimbursement, per unit, is going to get squeezed and your administrative costs are going to go up, your volume of patients can significantly increase.

So, essentially you're going to have to make it up in volume.

---

4 Groups of doctors, hospitals and other healthcare provid-ers who come together to provide coordinated high quality care to their Medicare patients.

You're going to have to see more patients. You're going to have to be more productive and efficient to make up for it.

How is Obamacare going to affect your staff clinicians?

Well, you're going to get squeezed here a little bit because of the lowered reimbursements and that may stifle their wages a bit.

Let's say you have a group plan right now and it goes up 30% next year. What are you going to do? You may have to take that cost increase in your group plan and then not be able to give the raise they might be expecting.

Health benefits are really just another form of compensation. If you pay $7,000.00 a year for your therapist to have health insurance you could just as easily have paid them the $7,000.00 in their salary. To you it's simply $7,000.00 that comes in the form of health insurance benefits.

You should educate your employees about this because you may not be able to raise their pay that much in the coming years ahead if your benefit costs are going to keep going up like this.

Another thing to consider is that health benefits are not as big an issue when competing for new clinicians to add to your team and that's a good thing. If you don't have a health plan now, when you're competing with other clinics that do have plans, your employees can go to the Marketplace and potentially get subsidized on their insurance plan getting the same coverage as the group plan at the clinic that you may be competing with.

There are a number of ways to work this to your advantage when hiring clinicians. So, keep this in mind as you work to expand your practice.

18
How Obamacare Will Affect You?

If you make a lot of money, you're going to pay more in taxes and the definition for "a lot of money" will keep changing because the government desperately needs money. There's not enough money in Obamacare to pay for all this "stuff."

Historically, the facts show that small business owners have had a much harder time providing themselves and their employees with insurance due to rising health insurance costs. Providers have had to deal with the complex and ever-changing reporting systems, decreasing reimbursement and more and more control over what is approved for billings.

As already discussed, while things are not going to get any easier under Obamacare, there is light at the end of this tunnel.

Quite a bit of it actually!

Don't become a victim to this complex evolution. New tools are both available and essential here because you want to be fully in control of your business, your employees, the services you provide to your patients and your continued expansion.

You can win this game if you know these rules. And this healthcare evolution can even be better for you in the end. It's loaded with opportunities.

You're going to have more patients with health insurance and more benefit options for your employees if you understand it and implement the right tools and strategies for it.

You should actually be getting ready for a higher volume of patients than you have now.

19
Obamacare Leverage Strategies

So, with all this information, what do we do to win this new healthcare game as an employer?

First of all, you can stay below 50 Full-Time Employees (FTEs) and avoid the health insurance mandate altogether. One of the ways that you can do that is to start creating other companies. There may be a number of ways to fully work this out.

Like anything else, the government comes up with new rules and the lawyers find the new loopholes. It will be a "cat and mouse" game to do this, but I believe people are going to do this left and right. So, think about that, but do get competent legal advice in advance to see if this strategy can work for you.

Stay below 50 Full-Time Employees (FTEs) as they are now defined (30 hours per week). That doesn't mean that you can't choose to offer group health insurance to your staff even if you are below the 50 FTEs, but it will be your own choice and you're not mandated to do so and you won't have to pay a penalty if you don't.

Stay under 50 and start looking at it now because as of July 1, 2013 the clock started ticking and don't forget, it's not where you were in January 2014, it's where you were on July 1, 2013.

You could really have a total of only 38 employees, but, because of the number of hours they actually work each week, it could officially be listed as 50 FTEs or more and you're toast. That's why you have to start calculating FTEs now.

Get with your CPA and run the numbers for your tax credits.

If you already have a group plan, it's going to have to conform to the Obamacare requirements; make sure it does.

Health Reimbursement Accounts (HRA)

This is a strategy you may be able to use by the way. The way a Health Reimbursement Account is supposed to work is that a company puts money into an HRA and then makes that money available to an employee to reimburse them for health-related expenses; and this even includes health insurance premiums.

So, for instance, if you have an employee who doesn't sign up for your group health insurance plan, you could put money each month into this HRA. The employee then goes to the Marketplace and gets health insurance coverage and then takes your $500.00 and put it towards that coverage.

That $500.00 to you is a routine business expense and for the employee it's a reimbursement, so it doesn't go through FICA (Federal Insurance Contributions Act) or Social Security. It's pre-tax. For those practices with less than 50 FTEs, who are already providing group health insurance this may be a good solution.

If you want to get out of this health insurance game you may be able to drop your group coverage and work out how much money you want to place into an HRA for all your employees and then let the subsidy in the Marketplace work for you.

If you have people that work for you where the government is going to subsidize their premiums and you're also going to subsidize it this way with your money, that employee will probably pay less money than they're now paying in your group plan and you'll be paying less money also. And you'll also be out of the health insurance business and avoid getting hit with 25% or 30% rate increases every year.

If your group plan gets hit and you want to get out of this game, then the Marketplace turns out to be a good thing. In other words, if the plans are good and the cost of them isn't through the roof and they're not viewed as being substandard, then this could be an excellent way for you to get out of the game altogether, while making sure that your employees are covered.

The Physical Therapist and Occupational Therapist Profession

As a Physical Therapist or Occupational Therapy professional here's a word of advice; you really need to get active with your associations.

Lobbying is everything now. You need to ensure that Physical Therapy and Occupational Therapy are included in the "essential benefits" at all times. To do so, you need to make sure that these therapies are being looked at as being part of the Obamacare "solution" and not part of the healthcare "problem" when it comes to results and reducing costs. If they fall lower and lower on the "totem pole" you may lose control over it. Remember, it's the government that's deciding what is or isn't essential now.

So, Physical Therapy and Occupational Therapy have to remain essential and I think they have a great chance of doing that.

Practice Owners

As a practice owner you must know the rules. This new health-care game will eat you alive if you don't know these rules.

Understand what the rules are and then just make the best economic decisions for your practice, your patients and your employees. You have a number of options which include: do nothing; wait and see; or even selling your business, none of which are likely going to be your best options.

Implement systems within your practice that enable you to help your patients and become a source of helpful information to them as they also navigate through the new healthcare system.

Examine your employee health insurance strategy—no insurance vs. group insurance vs. the Marketplace solutions.

Reimbursements

You should be diligent in getting paid. Make sure you apply the correct Current Procedural Terminology (CPT) code to get reimbursed. It's going to be so much more important to get paid and to stay on top of your billing staff to get paid every dime due because they're going to keep coming at you to try and lower your reimbursements.

20
Practice Metrics

Insurance carriers keep utilization data on every single provider. They use it for many purposes and they run their organization by the data they are able to obtain. With Electronic Health Records (EHR) you are pretty much forced to comply with their demands so that they can keep even better tabs on you.

You in turn keep track of a patient's condition with detailed objective information such as range of motion, strength and aerobic capacity among other data.

But, if you are not already doing so, it is very important that you keep careful numbers on your practice. This simple action alone will enable you to know things like; when is the right time to hire, where the practice may be losing money and whether or not you're actually doing better this week over last week.

All of my clients keep statistics. They plot them on graphs each week and then carefully analyze them and the inter-relationships of the various statistics throughout their practices in order to determine short and long-range strategies to better the condition of their organization on a week-to-week and month-to-month basis.

You know, for example, that if the number of calls coming into the practice each day is waning it may have something to do with the fact that no promotion has been going out for weeks. At an earlier time the phones were ringing off the hook and not, coincidently, just after the volume of promotion was at its highest.

This isn't rocket science, but you'd be surprised how many business owners don't keep the right statistics for their practice and when situations arise, they spend a lot of time trying to figure out what went wrong and what to do about it. Our clients don't have to. They know very quickly and can even predict and prevent situations from happening by just keeping the correct statistics. Better yet, they are able to CAUSE bettered conditions just by keeping and managing by the statistics they keep!

Below are a few key statistics that you should always keep and why.

Clinic Efficiencies

When we initially speak to a practitioner over the phone we need to know how many patients can actually be seen in their clinic each week. It is important to determine the potential, in patient volume of their practice within the confines of the physical space of the clinic itself.

If we spoke to a practitioner that saw only 100 patient visits a week in a 5,000 sq. ft. space then we would know that this practice would have significant potential to expand.

As a rule of thumb, regardless of how the space was organized or set up, a practice should see and treat 100 patients per week, per 1,000 sq. ft. of clinic space.

For example, if a practice has 3,000 sq. ft. we would expect a well-run and efficient practice to see 300 PVs a week in that space.

So, if your clinic has 3,000 sq. ft. and you were seeing 195 patients each week on average, then your clinic efficiency would be at 65%. 100% efficiency would be seeing 300 patients each week in a 3000 sq. ft. clinic.

In this example the facility's space itself would allow 105 more patient visits each week.

And if the reimbursement per visit was $85.00 a week then this practice should be able to generate an additional $8,925.00 a week or $464,100.00 annually from the existing 3,000 sq. ft. space if it were at capacity.

Too many practice owners open additional offices long before they've maximized the productivity potential of the facilities they already have.

Percent of Clinical Efficiency

This is simply the percentage of a full schedule on an average week for your clinicians.

For example, if you have 3 clinicians and you consider that they should be able to see 70 patients a week with a full schedule, then the ideal *Clinical Patient Volume* would be 210 patient visits per week. If, for example, the clinicians in a particular facility that should be operating at this volume were only seeing an average of 164 patients a week then the Clinical Efficiency would only be 78%. *Ideally your Clinical Efficiency should be 90% or above.*

What does this have to do with potential income?

Well in this scenario, if the average reimbursement per visit were $85.00 and the clinic was able to raise that statistic from 78% to 90% efficiency, the clinical staff already present could see 41 more patient visits and generate $3,442.50 additional income each week, which would be an additional $179,010.00 annually. By keeping a high clinical efficiency you can signifi-cantly lessen the financial blow Obamacare may create.

Clinical Efficiency is a good statistic to keep for *each* clinician and for the facility as a whole.

It is very common that there can be momentary demands for additional personnel, but if you were on top of this efficiency statistic and the clinic averaged 90% for a period of time, then you would know that you were ready to bring on another clinician while continuing to be viable.

Percentage of Kept Appointments vs. Percentage of Cancellations

When you plot or graph a statistic on a chart you always want an upwardly rising graph and that is why we also recommend that you keep a graphed statistic of the percentage of kept appointments and not your cancellation percentage.

A rising Percent of Kept Appointments statistic is a good thing and keeping this as a statistic enables you to go on keeping the statistic in a high range.

One of the first things we address with a new client is their *schedule book control*. If control in this area is poor, it is an indicator of a less than ideal practice management strategy.

We find that our clients who use our patient compliance system routinely get their percentage of kept appointments up to 95%.

The control at the front desk and working with the clinicians to get the percentage of kept appointments into a higher range is a very important routine action. It will become even more important as your patient co-pays and deductibles rise . . . because patients will attempt to self-regulate their care.

A practice that has an average of 200 patient visits a week with 40 cancellations, or no shows, has an 83% arrival rate. Now, if that same practice could get that arrival rate up to 95% they would make an additional $2,380.00 a week or $123,760.00 annually.

When you look at this amount of lost income you can see why we rapidly get our clients on our Patient Compliance Program as soon as possible to stop this income loss.

You should keep the percentage of kept appointments statistic on the total facility as well as each individual clinician.

Average Number of Visits per Patient per Week

This is the total patient visits per week divided by the number of unique patients seen that week.

For example; if you saw 200 patient visits one week and the total unique patients that week was 100 then the average number of visits per patient that week (ANVP/WK) would be two.

Clinicians will tend to self-regulate their productivity when they get busy and if you had a bunch of new patients coming in then you could end up seeing them less often per week because the clinician will make adjustments by scheduling those new patients fewer visits each week.

What you may end up with is a practice that has a high clinical efficiency, the clinician's schedule is full, but the statistic of Average Number of Patients per Visit per Week could be rapidly declining.

What is the ideal number for your clinic? Only you will have the answer to this, but as the patient's out-of-pocket rises, this statistic will likely decline so stay on top of it and I recommend that you keep this statistic for the facility and for each clinician as well.

Visits to Discharge

It is important to always stay on top of this particular statistic. We recommend that you look at this figure for the overall practice, but also look at it with each individual clinician.

You need to know that when a clinician begins to "go soft" with his or her control of their patient. It could be due to lack of know-how on handling a patient with a high out-of-pocket or just poor patient management style in general. When they begin to discharge early or the patient self-discharges, the practice, and the patient, <u>always</u> loses.

So keep the "Visits to Discharge" statistic. It will help to alert you before this gets too far out of hand.

Of course there are more metrics, but this is a good start for any practice.

If you are not managing your business by statistics and taking effective action . . . based upon the trends that they reveal . . . you could be losing bucket loads of money . . . and in a declining reimbursement environment this is something you cannot afford.

BONUS CHAPTER 1
The Healthcare Practitioner Transition Plan

Many years ago when I was in practice, capitation[5] was moving into the town. There were a couple of carriers that were intending to launch capitated insurance plans. As I began to research the pitfalls of being a provider under a capitated plan, I recognize that I would have to deliver my services differently in order to remain as viable as I had been.

I researched what I should be doing and implemented a program that would enable the patient to be seen, quality care continued to be delivered, and an active follow-up program initiated with patients over the phone to ensure that they were taking an active part in following through with their home exercise program. Establishment of this particular program was designed to lessen the number of visits that I would see the patient in the clinic yet still providing a good standard of care and remain viable.

---

5 Capitation (Definition) a payment method for healthcare services. The physician, hospital, or other healthcare provider is paid a contracted rate for each member assigned, referred to as "per-member-per-month" rate, regardless of the number or nature of services provided. Mosby's Medical Dictionary, 8th edition. © 2009

Fortunately, capitation never ended up coming in my city. Some might say that I was making preparations for no reason whatsoever, but I don't think so. I was making these changes because if they were to happen I wanted not to be hurt by them.

At that point in time, capitation was what I considered to be the practice killer. Having a capitated insurance plan and being paid enough outside of a fee-for-service model I thought would be catastrophic; so I took action.

What I was dealing with then is different now. Now we're going to be dealing with all carriers in the not-too-distant future putting the squeeze on us. So, now would also be the best time to start transitioning your practice for the eventuality of this changing healthcare environment.

When you have a direction you have certainty. If you're out in the ship at night wandering aimlessly without a compass, you are lost. To remain calm, you need to know where you are. From there you will need a heading, and of course, a compass. Only then could you have a plan. Once you have this you would then be able to take appropriate action to set a proper course for navigating these waters.

I have been studying the ACA for some time and just like when capitation was coming to town I was shocked at my peers who were not preparing. I would like to invite you to use the Healthcare Practitioner Transition Plan so that you are as prepared as you could be for what is to come.

Let's look at your lost income.

Lost income can be defined as the money that you could've made but you didn't. Many practice owners have been losing tons of money long before the ACA was even on the radar. Lost income is the most important area to address, so we will pay careful attention to that when creating your personalized ACA Transition Plan.

Your staff

Another area of your plan we address is the insuring of your staff. If you don't insure your staff now, how will you compete with larger corporations that do or must? If you are unable to insure everyone but wanted to hire a clinician how would you do it when he or she could get insurance coverage in a larger corporation with ease?

If you presently insure your staff, could there be a way to leverage the Exchanges and provide insurance coverage for a single staff member in the most economical way possible and lessen your overall tax burden? These questions and more are answered in the ACA Transition Plan.

The Healthcare Practitioner Transition Plan is our attempt to help you prepare.

You'll get a personalized report with a full breakdown of how to best insure your staff, how to better handle the patient with a high deductible who self-regulates their care and a careful assessment of your readiness to build up a cash-based service or cash practice.

You will also learn where you stand on key practice metrics and just how much income there is to recover in your practice right now and how to get it.

The Healthcare Practitioner Transition Plan is a two-step process

Step one: Contact our offices and set up an appointment for your personalized Healthcare Practitioner Transition Plan.

You will then be sent a simple form to fill out and fax back to our office.

Step two: We will review the information provided and, combined with your answers to our interview questions, generate your detailed and personalized plan.

Your personalized Healthcare Practitioner Transition Plan will be in the neighborhood of 10–13 pages and will be based upon the information you provide.

We will go over the plan with you over the phone and afterward email you your personalized practice Healthcare Practitioner Transition Plan and analytics that you will use to better your practice viability.

I encourage you to call and schedule your personalized Healthcare Practitioner Transition Plan. My company and my staff look forward to speaking with you and helping to ensure that private practices are here to stay and that they are viable and successful in the years to come.

You can call us at 800-491-2828 to schedule your Healthcare Practitioner Transition Plan or go to the following URL: www.MeasurableSolutions.com/TransitionPlan.

Glad to be of help!

BONUS CHAPTER 2
Timeline of Obamacare's Main Provisions

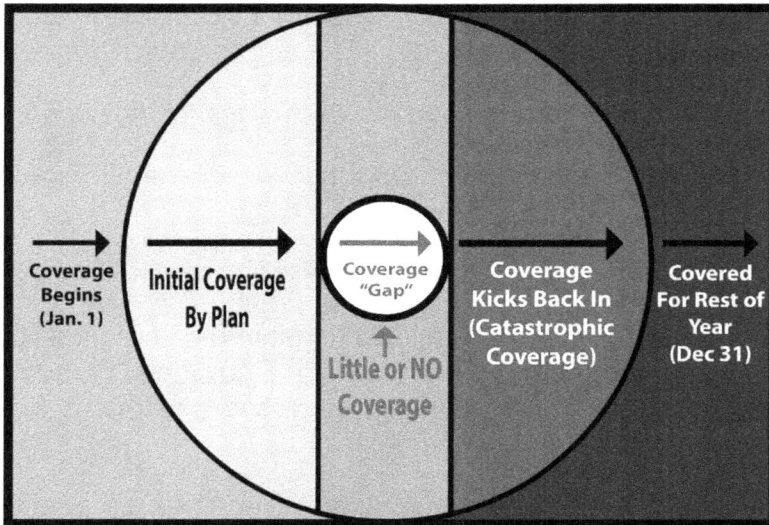

Coverage Begins (Jan. 1) → Initial Coverage By Plan → Coverage "Gap" (Little or NO Coverage) → Coverage Kicks Back In (Catastrophic Coverage) → Covered For Rest of Year (Dec 31)

OK, so now I am just going to walk you through the step-by-step roll out of Obamacare, year-by-year since 2010. I will go over what's already been implemented and what's going to be rolled out in the coming years.

When it first started, you might be aware of the "donut-whole" in the Medicare drug benefits where senior citizens could get financial help with their prescription drugs up to a certain limit. But, when they reached that limit, they'd get cut off. Then after a while they'd get some more help. So, there's sort of a hole in the middle of Medicare where there was no subsidy. Obamacare is supposed to eventually fill in that hole.

It started as a $250 tax credit and you should see that by 2020 this "hole" should be completely filled and seniors will have help in paying for all of their prescription drugs.

With Obamacare there will be no more lifetime limits on benefits. Insurance used to have a limit to lifetime benefits, but now they no longer do.

Your insurance can't be canceled except for fraudulent claims.

There's no cost-sharing for preventive in-network services so there's a lot more "free stuff." Well, it's not really free; you don't pay for it . . . at least not visibly where you might notice.

There are no pre-existing condition exclusions for kids under 19.

And your body tanning cost went up in 2010 when they added a 10% tax on it.

TIMELINE OF MAIN PROVISIONS—2011

In 2011 minimum Medical Loss Ratios for insurance companies were introduced and this is how it works:

Insurance companies get paid from insurance premiums paid to *them* by policyholders and they *pay out* in insurance claims or benefits. The Medical Loss Ratio is the difference between how much of that insurance company *income* is paid out in actual policyholder benefits as opposed to their administrative costs and profit.

The government is now going to decide what those ratios are, which essentially means that they're going to decide what insurance company profit margins will be. So, in a way, they're basically going to turn insurance companies into "utility" companies.

In 2011 a few more items were included on the prescription drugs and Medicare line.

Over the counter drugs would no longer be purchased with your Flexible Savings Accounts (FSAs) or your Health Savings Accounts (HSAs). You used to be able to get both prescription and over the counter drugs with these types of accounts, but you can't do that anymore. It now has to be prescription drugs only.

And then the first of a series of new fees charged to health-care providers and health device manufacturers began in 2011. These are really just new taxes on those companies behind-the-scenes that make the devices and machines that you ultimately use in your practice. So they'll also be taxed harder, which will get passed right on to you.

TIMELINE OF MAIN PROVISIONS—2012

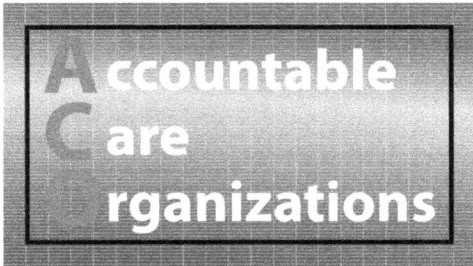

In 2012 the Accountable Care Organization or "ACO" essentially became the new term for those HMOs (Health Maintenance Organizations) from the 1970s.

This is where hospitals and healthcare providers come together and may be where you come in. You could get referred to from inside that network and while it may cost you less you'll have to stay inside it to benefit from it.

The most important point about this is the way the ACOs will work. They are going to get a flat amount of money to treat people and if they can treat people for less than what they get then they'll make a profit, if they can't then they won't make a profit.

There are a number of pilots that have been started on this and what you are going to have to figure out in your own geographic areas, as ACOs begin to take a foothold and grow, is whether you are "in" or you are "out." That's an evolution that probably won't fully complete for another two or three years into the Obamacare roll out, but you need to be aware of it.

Hospital re-admission rates will be hit hard. Every year hospitals with high re-admission rates are getting hit hard, but they are going to start getting hit even harder. You know, the patient comes back within thirty days after they were released. The hospital gets killed on penalties when this happens.

Wellness is going to be covered 100% almost everywhere as Obamacare moves forward. This could open up some huge opportunities for your practice. The healthcare law now allows employers to tether as much as 50% of workers' insurance costs to their participation in wellness programs. These can range, for example, from a reduced deductible for taking a health assessment to rewards for meeting a certain target weight or cholesterol level. The whole idea of workplace wellness programs is to give workers' a financial incentive to improve their health—or at least take certain preventive care steps they might otherwise skip.

Medical Loss Ratio

The "medical loss ratio" provision introduced in 2012 requires insurance companies to report insurance plan costs so that their medical loss ratios could be calculated. This is the percentage of insurance premium dollars spent on reimbursements for clinical services and other activities to improve healthcare quality.

Large group insurers are now required to spend at least 85% of their premium dollars on claims and activities to improve healthcare quality. Individual and small group insurers must spend at least 80% of premium dollars on this as well.

2012 was the first year, if you were an employee and you got health benefits from your employer-paid health insurance, the cost of those benefits now appeared on your W2 forms.

So, let's say it costs your employer $6,000.00 to give you your health benefit. It will be listed as $6,000.00 on your W2. It's just a memo type thing right now and you don't have to do anything with it. For now your health insurance benefit is a non-taxable thing, but it just may be the first step toward taxing insurance benefits.

TIMELINE OF MAIN PROVISIONS—2013

In 2013 the Adjusted Gross Income (AGI) of $200,000.00 as an individual or $250,000.00 as a family started getting hit with higher taxes.

And, it started with Medicare. Right now most of us pay 1.45% for our side of Medicare taxes and your company pays 1.45%. There is an actual 0.9% that goes on top of that if you exceed this salary range.

And then a 3.8% increase in unearned income went into effect, which included stock dividends, bank interest and any other income that was not part of an individual's normal wages. So, if you make more than $200,000.00 or $250,000.00 you will get hit with 3.8% more in taxes and all of this is supposed to go to fund Obamacare.

You may be familiar with the Flexible Savings Accounts or FSAs that were briefly discussed earlier. These are a type of savings account available in the United States that provide employers with specific tax advantages. Set up by the employer, this type of account allows employees to contribute a portion of their regular earnings to pay for qualified expenses such as medical expenses or dependent care costs.

Well, the amount of money allowed to be placed by the employer into an FSA is now being significantly reduced and limited. They used to allow as much as $5,000.00; they're now down to $2,500.00. The government is now, in effect, pushing you away from Flexible Savings Accounts.

2013 also introduced a 2.3% excise tax on medical devices. Actually some legislators have put a bill into the Senate to make it go away, which is what usually happens in this type of scenario. A legislator puts a tax bill on the lines and, when they actually try to implement it, any state that has a significant medical device company in it that doesn't want the new tax bill to go through starts to lobby and debate against it.

If this new excise tax survives it just means that your device products and insurance premiums will be higher because they will just pass the tax costs along to the consumer.

On a personal note, if you itemized your medical deductions under your taxes in the past, the threshold to do that went up to 10%. It was 7.5% so you get hit a little there as well.

TIMELINE OF MAIN PROVISIONS—2014

We are well into 2014 and Obamacare has already had a very big year. This is the year that the new "Health Insurance Marketplace" appeared online along with the new insurance premium subsidies for qualified participants.

Originally, this was the year that the individual insurance mandate was to have started. The government said; "You had to get insurance or you have to pay a $285.00 fine." But that changed toward the end of 2013 and the mandate and the fines were put off another year . . . so far. We'll see what happens here as Obamacare moves on.

This is also the year that insurance was guaranteed to be issued and guaranteed renewable.

What this essentially means is that you are going to get insurance now that can't be taken away from you no matter what happens to you. And you're guaranteed to have certain essential benefits inside that insurance policy.

As of 2014 there are no more annual benefit limits. "Essential Benefits" took effect. Obamacare requires all health insurance plans sold after 2014 to include a basic package of essential benefits including; hospitalization, outpatient services, maternity care, prescription drugs, emergency care and preventive services among other benefits. Again, this can open up significant service opportunities for you and your practice.

There is a new small business tax credit. If you're a small business right now and you have a group health plan then you may be eligible for tax credits to help pay for that plan. You should check into that immediately if you are providing health insurance to your employees.

Despite all of the technological hiccups and significant changes already announced or fully or even partially implemented, the government claims that the administration of this healthcare system is going to be much simpler . . . *and we can't wait for that.*

TIMELINE OF MAIN PROVISIONS—2015–2020

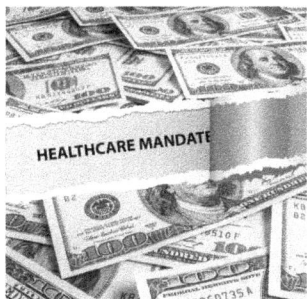

Whenever they actually implement and enforce the insurance mandate, in 2015 we're told the penalty for not getting insurance will go up to $975.00 for each individual who opts not to get a health insurance plan and does not already have one through his or her employer. In 2016 it is will increase to $2,085.

By 2017 the Insurance Marketplace will be opened for large companies to obtain large insurance plans.

The Independent Payment Advisory Board, or IPAB, is a fifteen-member United States Government agency that was created in 2010 by the Patient Protection and Affordable Care

Act. It has the explicit task of achieving significant savings in Medicare without affecting coverage or quality.

Under previous and current law any changes to Medicare payment rates or program rules required an act of Congress to take effect. Obamacare established that the Independent Payment Advisory Board (IPAB) will have full authority to make changes to the Medicare program and Congress was only given the power to overrule the agency's decisions through a supermajority three-fifths vote.

During this time period the IPAB starts making cost effective, cost reducing treatment "recommendations."

In 2020 IPAB's recommendations become law unless over-ruled by a supermajority congressional vote.

And by 2020, your Medicare prescription drug "Donut Hole" for the elderly is to be filled.

Glossary

A

Accountable Care Organization (ACO)—Groups of doctors, hospitals and other healthcare providers who come together to provide coordinated high quality care to their Medicare patients. The Affordable Care Act's most significant contribution to creating ACOs is in the traditional Medicare fee-for-service system. The law includes a provision that allows Medicare to reward healthcare organizations with a share of the savings that would result from improving care quality and reducing the cost for their eligible Medicare populations.

Actuarial Value—Actuarial value is often seen as the "true" value of a plan. It is the percentage of covered costs that the plan expects to pay for an enrollee in the plan. For example; a person with a plan that had an actuarial value of 70% would then be responsible for the remaining 30% of the cost of the covered benefits under the plan.

Until the passage of ACA, "actuarial value" was not a household term. Long-time insurance employees likely have a loose grasp on the concept, but in the post-reform world, it will be a commonly used tool to estimate the true value of a plan.

Adjusted Gross Income (AGI)—In the United States income tax system, adjusted gross income (AGI) is measure of income used to determine how much of your income is taxable. Adjusted gross income (AGI) is calculated as your gross income from taxable sources minus allowable deductions, such as unreimbursed business expenses,medical expenses, alimony and deductible retirement plan contributions.

Affordability Test—Health insurance coverage is deemed to be affordable for the Patient Protection and Affordability Act purposes if the cost to the employee of *self-only coverage* does not exceed 9.5% of the employees "household income." This is so irrespective of whether he or she qualifies for some other level of coverage (e.g., self-plus dependents, family). Thus, despite that family coverage might require a larger employee premium, affordability for is determined based on the cost of self-only coverage. The Act further defines "household income" to mean "modified adjusted gross income of the employee and any members of the employee's family (including a spouse and dependents) who are required to file an income tax return." Recognizing the fact that many employers would generally not know or care to know their employees' total household incomes, the regulations permit employers to use one of three safe harbors as proxies: W-2, rate-of-pay or Federal Poverty Line.

Affordable Care Act (ACA)—The Patient Protection and Affordable Care Act (PPACA), commonly called the Affordable Care Act (ACA) or "Obamacare," is a United States federal statute regarding healthcare that was signed into law by President Barack Obama on March 23, 2010.

C

Capitation—*noun.* A payment method for healthcare services. The physician, hospital, or other healthcare provider is paid a contracted rate for each member assigned, referred to as "per-member-per-month" rate, regardless of the number or nature of services provided.

Clinic Efficiencies—The relationships between what a clinic could and should be able to produce collectively taking its available space and resources into account and comparing it to what it actually does produce during any given time frame.

Current Procedural Terminology (CPT)—A listing of descriptive terms and identifying codes for reporting medical services and procedures. The purpose of such terminology is to provide a uniform language for healthcare practitioners, patients, and third parties.

E

Electronic Health Records (EHR)—An electronic health record (EHR) is a digital version of a patient's paper chart. EHRs are real-time, patient-centered records that make information available instantly and securely to authorized users.

Electronic Medical Records (EMR)—An electronic medical record (EMR) is a digital version of a paper chart that contains all of a patient's medical history from one practice. An EMR is mostly used by providers for diagnosis and treatment.

Employer Mandate—The Obamacare "employer mandate" is a requirement that all businesses with over 50 full-time or full-time equivalent (FTE) employees provide health insurance for their full-time employees, or pay a fine each month known as the "Employer Shared Responsibility Payment" on their federal tax return. Originally set to begin in 2014, the Employer Mandate will be delayed until 2015 / 2016.

Employer Mandate Update—Small businesses with 50-99 full-time equivalent employees (FTE) will need to start insuring workers by 2016. Those with a 100 or more will need to start providing health benefits to at least 70% of their FTE by 2015 and 95% by 2016. Healthcare tax credits have been retroactively available to small businesses with 25 or less full-time equivalent employees since 2010.

Essential Health Benefits—The Patient Protection and Affordable Care Act placed certain coverage requirements on essential health benefits, and provides a broad set of benefit categories that would be considered essential to a health benefits package—including hospitalization, outpatient services, emergency care, prescription drugs, maternity, etc.

Exchange (State Insurance Exchange)—Obamacare, AKA the Affordable Care Act, implements State specific health insurance exchanges which are online price comparison websites where consumers can purchase health insurance. Open enrollment in all marketplaces initially went from October 1, 2013 to March 31, 2014. These are resources where individuals, families, and small businesses can: learn about their health coverage options; compare health insurance plans based on costs, benefits, and other important features; choose a plan; and enroll in coverage.

F

Federal Poverty Line—The set minimum amount of gross income that a family needs for food, clothing, transportation, shelter and other necessities. In the United States, this level is determined by the Department of Health and Human Services. The most current Federal Poverty Line numbers for individuals and families is listed on the U.S. Department of Health & Human Services web site: http://aspe.hhs.gov/poverty/14poverty.cfm.

Flexible Savings Account (FSA)—A type of savings account available in the United States that provides the account holder with specific tax advantages. Set up by an employer for an employee, the account allows employees to contribute a portion of their regular earnings to pay for qualified expenses, such as medical expenses or dependent care expenses.

FTE (Full-time/Full-time Equivalent Employee)—In the U.S. federal government, FTE is defined by the Government Accountability Office (GAO) as the number of total hours worked divided by the maximum number of compensable hours in a full-time schedule as defined by law. Prior to the passage of the Patient Protection and Affordability Act a full-time employee was considered to work an average 40 hour week. With the passage of the new healthcare law, an individual who works an average 30-hours per week is now considered a full-time or full-time equivalent employee.

H

Health Insurance Exchange—A resource where individuals, families, and small businesses can: learn about their health coverage options; compare health insurance plans based on costs, benefits, and other important features; choose a plan; and enroll in coverage. The Marketplace also provides information on programs that help people with low to moderate income and resources pay for coverage. This includes ways to save on the monthly premiums and out-of-pocket costs of coverage available through the Marketplace, and information about other programs, including Medicaid and the Children's Health Insurance Program (CHIP). The Marketplace encourages competition among private health plans, and is accessible through websites, call centers, and in-person assistance. In some states, the Marketplace is run by the state. In others it is run by the federal government.

Health Insurance Subsidies—Many Americans will receive premium tax credits to help offset the costs of insurance under the healthcare reform law. These tax credits are available to people who don't get what is considered affordable, comprehensive health insurance coverage through their employers and whose household income is less than 400% of the federal poverty level, which in 2014 is about $46,000 for an individual, or about $78,000 for a family of three.

Health Reimbursement Accounts (HRA)—Employer-funded plans that reimburse employees for incurred medical expenses that are not covered by the company's standard insurance plan. Because the employer funds the plan, any distributions are considered tax deductible to the employer. Reimbursement dollars received by the employee are also generally tax free.

Higher Deductibles—A health insurance plan that has a high minimum deductible, which does not cover the initial costs or all of the costs of medical expenses.

Health Savings Account (HSA)—A savings account used in conjunction with a high-deductible health insurance policy that allows users to save money tax-free against medical expenses.

I

Independent Payment Advisory Board (IPAB)—In 2010, the Patient Protection and Affordable Care Act authorized the creation of the Independent Payment Advisory Board (IPAB) to help control the growth in Medicare costs. It is a fifteen-member United States Government agency created in 2010 by sections 3403 and 10320 of the Patient Protection and Affordable Care Act which has the explicit task of achieving specified savings in Medicare without affecting coverage or quality. Under previous and current law, changes to Medicare payment rates and program rules are recommended by MedPAC but require an act of Congress to take effect. Beginning in 2014, IPAB will issue recommendations to lower Medicare costs in the event that spending exceeds targets established in the healthcare reform law.

Individual Mandate—Beginning in 2014, the Affordable Care Act includes a mandate for most individuals to have health insurance or potentially pay a penalty for noncompliance. Individuals will be required to maintain minimum essential coverage for themselves and their dependents. Some individuals will be exempt from the mandate or the penalty, while others may be given financial assistance to help them pay for the cost of health insurance.

Insurance Marketplace—Organizations that facilitate structured and competitive markets for purchasing health coverage. The Health Insurance Marketplace, or "Exchange," offers standardized health insurance plans to individuals, families and small businesses.

M

Mandate—Mandated health insurance is when one is legally required to purchase health insurance or suffer fines for not doing so. This is the term most often used in the new health insurance reform legislation by the Obama administration.

Marketplace—Organizations that facilitate structured and competitive markets for purchasing health coverage. The Health Insurance Marketplace, or "Exchange," offers standardized health insurance plans to individuals, families and small businesses.

Medicaid—Created when President Lyndon B. Johnson signed amendments to the Social Security Act on July 30, 1965, Medicaid is a U.S. government program that is financed by federal, state and local taxes for the hospitalization and medical insurance for persons within certain income limits. Medicaid is the largest source of funding for medical and health-related services for people with low income in the United States.

Medical Loss Ratios—The percent of premium an insurer spends on claims and expenses that improve healthcare quality.

Medicare—In the United States, Medicare is a national social insurance program, administered by the U.S. federal government since 1966, that guarantees access to health insurance for Americans aged 65 and older who have worked and paid into the system, and younger people with disabilities, as well as people with end-stage renal disease and persons with amyotrophic lateral sclerosis. As a social insurance program, Medicare spreads the financial risk associated with illness across society to protect everyone, and thus has a somewhat different social role from for-profit private insurers, which manage their risk portfolio by adjusting their pricing according to perceived risk.

Medicare Advantage—(MA) A type of Medicare health plan offered by a private company that contracts with Medicare to provide you with all your Part A and Part B benefits. Medicare Advantage Plans include Health Maintenance Organizations (HMOs), Preferred Provider Organizations (PPOs), Private Fee-for-Service Plans, Special Needs Plans, and Medicare Medical Savings Account Plans. For people enrolled in a Medicare Advantage Plan Medicare services are covered through the plan itself and aren't paid for under Original Medicare. Most Medicare Advantage Plans also offer prescription drug coverage.

O

Obamacare—AKA "The Patient Protection and Affordable Care Act" and "The Affordable Care Act," Obamacare is a federal law providing for the fundamental reform of the U.S. healthcare and health insurance system, at reforming the American healthcare system.

P

Patient Protection and Affordable Care Act (PPACA)—The Patient Protection and Affordable Care Act (PPACA), commonly called the Affordable Care Act (ACA) or "Obamacare," is a United States federal statute regarding healthcare that was signed into law by President Barack Obama on March 23, 2010.

Practice Metrics—The management process used by owners and managers in which to evaluate various aspects of their practice in relation to objectives and accomplishments. Tracking key production statistics regularly enables organizations to develop and implement plans to recover from failures, implement immediate and longer range improvements, predict future outcomes and adapt specific best practices, usually with the aim of increasing some aspect of performance. This type of benchmarking is often treated as a continuous process in which organizations continually seek to improve their practices.

Premium Subsidies—Many Americans will receive premium tax credits to help offset the costs of insurance under the healthcare reform law. These tax credits are available to people who don't get what is considered affordable, comprehensive health insurance coverage through their employers and whose household income is less than 400 percent of the federal poverty level, which in 2014 is about $46,000 for an individual, or about $78,000 for a family of three.

Premium Tax Credits—The premium tax credit is an advanceable, refundable tax credit designed to help eligible individuals and families with low or moderate income afford health insurance purchased through the Health Insurance Marketplace, also known as the Exchange, beginning in 2014.

R

Romneycare—Healthcare plans instituted by the state of Massachusetts under the governorship of Mitt Romney, which provided for complete coverage of all citizens of the Commonwealth, and included an individual mandate to purchase health insurance for those able to pay.

S

Social Security Amendments—An entitlement program to help states provide medical coverage for low-income families and other categorically related individuals who meet eligibility requirements.

State (Insurance) Exchange—Obamacare, AKA the Affordable Care Act, implements State specific health insurance exchanges which are online price comparison websites where consumers can purchase health insurance. Open enrollment in all marketplaces initially went from October 1, 2013 to March 31, 2014.

U

Universal Coverage—Universal coverage (UC), or universal health coverage (UHC), is defined as ensuring that all people can use the promotive, preventive, curative, rehabilitative and palliative health services they need, of sufficient quality to be effective, while also ensuring that the use of these services does not expose the user to financial hardship—*defined by the World Health Organization (WHO)*

W

Workers Compensation (noun)—A system of insurance that reimburses an employer for damages that must be paid to an employee for injury occurring in the course of employment—called also workers' comp.

Acknowledgments

I would like to acknowledge my partner for his continuous support. Fifteen years ago we were two guys in a garage with an idea. That idea was to enhance the survival of independent practice. Today we have helped greater than 2,500 private practices throughout the US and Canada and have been a very positive influence in the long-term viability of the independent private practitioner.

I would like to thank my wife, Peggy. As I became more successful in my physical therapy practice, I leveraged my free time to help others with their businesses just for fun. I like to help able people become more and more able and she saw what was happening in me. When I told her I wanted to sell my practice to start a management training and consulting company, it was without hesitation she completely understood and supported me. I will forever love her for that.

I would like to thank Steve Masie, MBA for delivering a seminar on the impact of Obamacare to our clients that lit the spark and inspired me to research and study the Patient Protection and Affordable Care Act and write this book.

I would also like to thank Rudi C. Loehwing for being such an excellent "Task Master" and pushing me to write this book to benefit all healthcare practioners and not just my clients.

Margie Rosenstein, thank you for lending your artistic talent to the creation of the perfect cover design for this important work.

Thank you to Ginger Marks, of DocUmeantDesigns.com, both for included graphics and your talent and expertice in making this book attractive on the inside; you are warmly thanked and acknowledged for your creative talents.

Notes

Chapter 2

The Patient Protection and Affordable Care Act—available in full from the U.S. Government Printing Office—http://www.gpo.gov A full copy of the PPACA is available at this link: http://www.gpo.gov/fdsys/pkg/BILLS-111hr3590enr/pdf/BILLS-111hr3590enr.pdf

Chapter 3

CNN: "The U.S. Supreme Court's ruling upholding the healthcare law championed by President Barack Obama reignited an intense debate, with Democrats celebrating millions of Americans getting access to insurance while Republicans railed against what they contend is a dangerous expansion of government."—Full CNN Coverage: http://www.cnn.com/2012/06/28/politics/supreme-court-health-ruling/

Chapter 4

Surtax on Investment Income—Bill: Reconciliation Act; Page 87—93

Hike in Medicare Payroll Tax—Bill: PPACA, Reconciliation Act; Page: 2000—2003; 87—93

Tax on Health Insurers—Bill: PPACA, Page 1,986—1,993

Excise Tax on Comprehensive Health Insurance Plans—Bill: PPACA, Page: 1,941—1,956

"Black Liquor" Tax Hike—Bill: Reconciliation Act; Page 105

Tax on Innovative Drug Companies— Bill: PPACA; Page 1,971—1,980

Tax on Medical Device Manufacturers—Bill: PPACA; Page 1,980—1,986

High Medical Bills Tax—Bill: PPACA; Page 1,994—1,995

Flexible Savings Account Cap—aka "Special Needs Kids Tax"—Bill: PPACA; Page 2,388—2,389

Medicine Cabinet Tax—Bill: PPACA; Page 1,957—1,959

Elimination of tax deduction for employer-provided retirement Rx drug coverage—Bill: PPACA; Page 1994

Codification of the "economic substance doctrine"—Bill: Reconciliation Act; Page 108—113

Tax on Indoor Tanning Services—Bill: PPACA; Page 2,397—2,399

HSA Withdrawal Tax Hike—Bill: PPACA; Page: 1,959

$500,000 Annual Executive Compensation Limit for Health Insurance Executives—Bill: PPACA; Page: 1,995—2,000

Blue Cross / Blue Shield Tax Hike—Bill: PPACA; Page: 2004

Excise Tax on Charitable Hospitals—Bill: PPACA; Page: 1,961—1,971

Employer Reporting of Insurance on W-2—Bill: PPACA; Page: 1,957

IRS—Changes to Itemized Deduction for
2013 Medical Expenses; http://www.irs.gov/
Individuals/2013-Changes-to-Itemized-Deduction-for-Medical-Expenses

Chapter 5

Obamacare Facts: "Facts on the Affordable Care Act"—http://
obamacarefacts.com/obamacare-facts.php

The Patient Protection and Affordable Care Act (full copy)—http://www.
gpo.gov/fdsys/pkg/BILLS-111hr3590enr/pdf/BILLS-111hr3590enr.pdf

Democratic Policy and Communications Committee—http://www.dpcc.
senate.gov/ "The Patient Protection and Affordable Care Act: Detailed
Summary"—http://www.dpc.senate.gov/healthreformbill/healthbill04.pdf

Chapter 6

Obamacare Facts: "How Will Obamacare Affect Me? What Obamacare Means for You, Your Family, and Your Business"—http://obamacarefacts. com/how-will-obamacare-affect-me.php

Chapter 7

Medicare.Gov: "Cost in Coverage Gap"—http://www.medicare.gov/ part-d/costs/coverage-gap/part-d-coverage-gap.html

AARP.Org: "Donut Hole Calculator"—http://doughnuthole.aarp.org/ Forbes Magazine: "Obamacare: Seven Major Provisions And How They Affect You"—http://www.forbes.com/sites/mikepatton/2013/11/27/ how-obamacare-will-change-the-american-health-system/

Chapter 8

The Center for Consumer Information & Insurance Oversight: "Medical Loss Ratio" -http://www.cms.gov/CCIIO/Programs-and-Initiatives/Health-Insurance-Market-Reforms/Medical-Loss-Ratio.html

IRS.Org: Flexible Savings Accounts (FSAs), Health Savings Accounts (HSAs)—http://www.irs.gov/publications/p969/ar02.html

Chapter 9

Centers for Medicare and Medicaid Services: "Accountable Care Organizations (ACO)"—http://www.cms. gov/Medicare/Medicare-Fee-for-Service-Payment/ACO/

Accountable Care Facts: "America's Accountable Care Organizations"— http://www.accountablecarefacts.org/

Chapter 10

IRS.gov: "Definition of Adjusted Gross Income"—http://www.irs.gov/uac/ Definition-of-Adjusted-Gross-Income

Healthcare.gov: "Modified Adjusted Gross Income"—http://www.irs.gov/ uac/Definition-of-Adjusted-Gross-Income

Healthcare.gov: "What is an FSA?"—https://www.healthcare.gov/ can-i-use-a-flexible-spending-account-fsa/

Chapter 11

Healthcare.gov: "Essential Health Benefits"—https://www.healthcare.gov/glossary/essential-health-benefits/

Healthcare.gov: "10 healthcare benefits covered in the Health Insurance Marketplace"—https://www.healthcare.gov/blog/10-health-care-benefits-covered-in-the-health-insurance-marketplace/

Chapter 12

Obamacare Employer Mandate—http://obamacarefacts.com/obamacare-employer-mandate.php

Healthcare.gov: "What if I don't have health coverage?"—https://www.healthcare.gov/what-if-i-dont-have-health-coverage/

Healthcare.gov: "What is the Employer Shared Responsibility Payment?"—https://www.healthcare.gov/what-is-the-employer-shared-responsibility-payment/

Healthcare.gov: "Businesses have new requirements under the new Healthcare law. Learn your options for protecting your business and employees"—https://www.healthcare.gov/businesses/

Chapter 13

Whitehouse.gov: "Healthcare that Works for Americans"—http://www.whitehouse.gov/healthreform

Forbes Magazine: The Three Types of Universal Healthcare

World Health Organization: "What is Universal Health Coverage?"—http://www.who.int/health_financing/universal_coverage_definition/en/

Healthcare.gov: "What if I don't have health coverage?"—https://www.healthcare.gov/what-if-i-dont-have-health-coverage/

Healthcare.gov: "What is the Employer Shared Responsibility Payment?"—https://www.healthcare.gov/what-is-the-employer-shared-responsibility-payment/

Healthcare.gov: "Businesses have new requirements under the new Healthcare law. Learn your options for protecting your business and employees"—https://www.healthcare.gov/businesses/

Chapter 14

Healthcare.gov: "Get Covered: A one-page guide to the Health Insurance Marketplace"—https://www.healthcare.gov/get-covered-a-1-page-guide-to-the-health-insurance-marketplace/

Chapter 15

Healthcare.gov: "Essential Health Benefits"—https://www.healthcare.gov/glossary/essential-health-benefits/

Chapter 16

Obamacarefacts.com: "State Health Insurance Exchange: State Run Exchanges"—http://obamacarefacts.com/state-health-insurance-exchange.php

Washington Post: Supreme Court Ruling on Obamacare (full text) — http://www.washingtonpost.com/wp-srv/politics/documents/supreme-court-health-care-decision-text.html

Chapter 17

National Review: 'Remember When State Obamacare Exchanges Were the Good Ones?'—http://www.nationalreview.com/corner/379533/remember-when-state-obamacare-exchanges-were-good-ones-veronique-de-rugy

Chapter 18

Healthcare.gov: "7 ways to save in the Health Insurance Marketplace"—https://www.healthcare.gov/blog/7-ways-to-save-in-the-health-insurance-marketplace/

Healthcare.gov: "Will I qualify for lower costs on monthly premiums?"—https://www.healthcare.gov/will-i-qualify-to-save-on-monthly-premiums/

The Henry J. Kaiser Family Foundation: "Health Insurance Subsidy Calculator"—http://kff.org/interactive/subsidy-calculator/

Chapter 19

Medicare.gov: "What Medicare covers"—http://www.medicare.gov/what-medicare-covers/index.html

Medicaid.gov: "Medicaid"—http://www.medicare.gov/your-medicare-costs/help-paying-costs/medicaid/medicaid.html

Association of American Medical Colleges: "The Independent Payment Advisory Board (IPAB)"—https://www.aamc.org/advocacy/medicare/153896/independent_payment_advisory_board_ipab.html

Cornell University Law School: "Title 42 › Chapter 7 Subchapter XVIII Part E § 1395kkk 42 U.S. Code § 1395kkk—Independent Payment Advisory Board"—http://www.law.cornell.edu/uscode/text/42/1395kkk

Chapter 20

Medicare.gov: "Medicare Advantage Plans"—http://www.medicare.gov/sign-up-change-plans/medicare-health-plans/medicare-advantage-plans/medicare-advantage-plans.html

Chapter 21

Healthcare.gov: "Full-time Equivalent (FTE) Employee Calculator"—https://www.healthcare.gov/shop-calculators-fte/

IRS.gov: " Determining FTEs and Average Annual Wages" -

http://www.irs.gov/uac/Small-Business-Health-Care-Tax-Credit-Questions-and-Answers:-Determining-FTEs-and-Average-Annual-Wages

Medicalmutual.com: "Minimum Value Define"—https://www.medmutual.com/For-Employers/Healthcare-Reform/Affordable-Care-Act-Summary/HCR-Items/Minimum-Value-Defined.aspx

Medicalmutual.com: "Actuarial Value Defined"—https://www.medmutual.com/For-Employers/Healthcare-Reform/Affordable-Care-Act-Summary/HCR-Items/Actuarial-Value-Defined.aspx

Chapter 22

Forbes: "Obamacare Deductibles Hit Patient Pocketbooks And Hospital Finances"—http://www.forbes.com/sites/brucejapsen/2014/02/22/obamacare-deductibles-hit-patient-pocketbooks-and-hospital-finances/

Healthcare.gov: "Rehabilitative services and devices under Obamacare"—http://obamacarefacts.com/essential-health-benefits.php

Centers for Medicare and Medicaid Services: "The Affordable Care Act: Lowering Medicare Costs by Improving Care"—http://www.cms.gov/apps/files/aca-savings-report-2012.pdf

Chapter 23

Centers for Medicare and Medicaid Services: "Accountable Care Organizations (ACO)"—http://www.cms.gov/Medicare/Medicare-Fee-for-Service-Payment/ACO/

Accountable Care Facts: "America's Accountable Care Organizations"—http://www.accountablecarefacts.org/

Chapter 24

Centers for Medicare and Medicaid Services: "Accountable Care Organizations (ACO)"—http://www.cms.gov/Medicare/Medicare-Fee-for-Service-Payment/ACO/

The Cato Institute: "Let's Look at Romneycare"—http://www.cato.org/publications/commentary/lets-look-romneycare?print

Index

A

ACA
  Affordable Care Act 1, 3, 4, 5, 6, 8, 11, 15, 17, 67, 69, 70, 71, 72, 74, 76, 81, 82, 87
ACO
  Accountable Care Organization 63, 69
Actuarial Value 37, 69, 86
Affordability Test 36, 70
AGI
  Adjusted Gross Income 65, 69

C

Capitation 57, 70
Clinic Efficiencies 52, 70
CPT
  Current Procedural Terminology 50, 71

E

EHR 51, 71
  Electronic Health Records 51, 71
Employer Mandate 11, 71, 84
Employer's Choice 34
EMR
  Electronic Medical Records 42, 71
Essential Health Benefits 20, 71, 84, 85
Exchange (State Insurance Exchange) 72

F

Federal Poverty Line 28, 29, 32, 70, 72
FSA
  Flexible Savings Account 11, 72, 82
FTE
  Full Time/Full Time Equivalent Employee 34, 71, 72, 86

H

Healthcare Practitioner Transition Plan 57, 58, 59, 60
Health Insurance Exchange 8, 73, 85

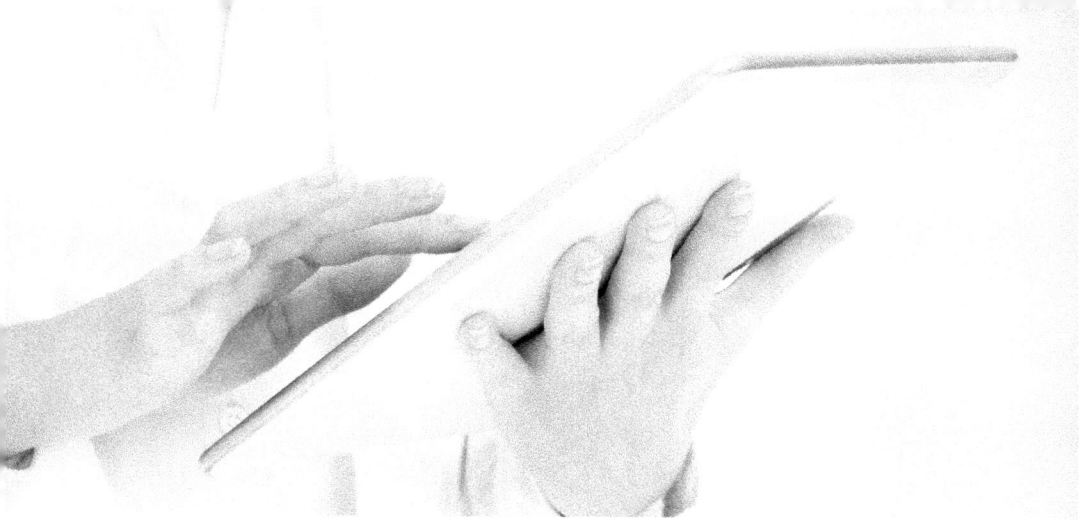

THE HEALTHCARE PRACTITIONER TRANSITION PLAN

The longer you wait to see what happens with Obamacare without making any adjustments in your business practice the deeper the hole you may have to pull yourself out of.

No matter what happens with Obamacare there are key things that you will continue to be prepared for:

• Continued decreases in reimbursements = getting paid less per patient.

• Higher deductibles means your patients will be paying more out of pocket.

• Patients will begin to self discharge early to save money.

Get your FREE Healthcare Practitioner Transition Plan and find out:

• Where your clinic stands on proven Practice Metrics

• How much lost income there is to recover and

• How to get at it right now!

COMPLETE YOUR FREE HEALTHCARE PRACTITIONER TRANSITION PLAN ONLINE:
www.MeasurableSolutions.Com/TransitionPlan
OR **CALL 800-491-2828** to have one sent to via email

MEASURABLE
SOLUTIONS

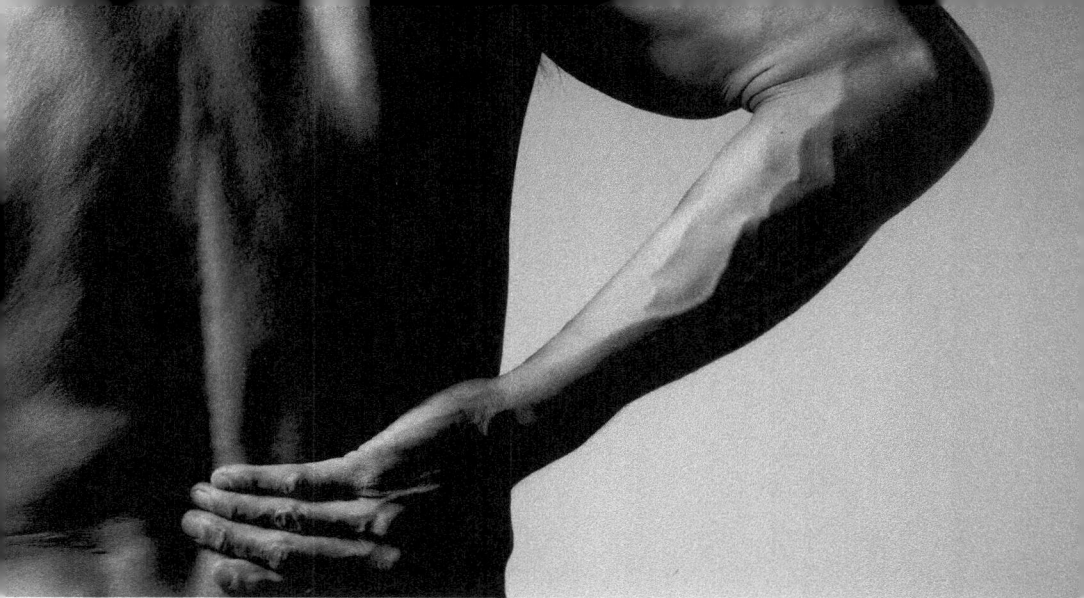

www.ingramcontent.com/pod-product-compliance
Lightning Source LLC
Chambersburg PA
CBHW071528200326

41519CB00019B/6117